In Praise of SIMPLY SPIRIT

I found myself taking frequent breaks to contemplate, reflect and journal on the thought-provoking words of Joseph Eliezer. I could hear and feel his soul through his loving and non-judgmental words. I found myself questioning the very essence of my being and just how and who to "be" in the world. This book strengthens the "inner being" and builds confidence in your personal intuition. It is an "immortal" book that I will reflect upon often as I continue along my spiritual journey.

— Jivi Khehra, TV Host of *Winds of Change with Jivi*

A deeply personal and soul-stirring work offering wisdom and insight into many facets of life – from money and success to elements of the spiritual journey.

Joseph writes simply and straight from the soul, challenging and beckoning without preaching or patronizing. Joseph's voice speaks directly and deeply and he doesn't underestimate his readers' intelligence or spiritual capacity by spelling it all out for us. The reader is given enough room to glean meaning that is relevant for his or her unique journey of personal and spiritual work.

These treasures will stand the test of time and reveal new layers of meaning with each fresh read, encouraging us to look deeply into ourselves and explore our inner process and our soul's journey.

In a time when New Age books and teachings are bombarding us with insistent directives about how to manage our spiritual lives, this book is a refreshing and welcome invitation.

— Mahalia Eliah, Spiritual Emergence Service

Just when I thought I had seen it all, read it all and heard it all in the realm of spiritual literature, I came across Simply Spirit *by Joseph Eliezer. Unapologetic and edgy, yet deeply comforting and inspiring, this book jolted me into a whole new level of consciousness. I love it here.*

— Liora Steiman, MD, MEd in Couns. Psych., Therapist

Words by Joseph: Book One

SIMPLY SPIRIT

A Personal Guide to Spiritual Clarity
One Insight at a Time

JOSEPH ELIEZER

Agio
PUBLISHING HOUSE

I am the stars that shine so bright.
I am the sun that beams delight.
I am the moon that illuminates the night.
I am the Spirit and I am the Light.

Why are you different than I am?

151 Howe Street, Victoria BC Canada V8V 4K5

For rights information and bulk orders, please contact:
info@agiopublishing.com or go to
www.agiopublishing.com

Simply Spirit
ISBN 978-1-897435-42-7 (trade paperback)

Author's website
www.1111spiritroad.com

Printed on acid-free paper. Agio Publishing House is a
socially responsible company, measuring success on a
triple-bottom-line basis.

10 9 8 7 6 5 4 3 2 1

This book is dedicated
to the memory of my aunt Mary,
whose love, warmth and decency
still remain with me long after her passing.

A Special Acknowledgement
To my partner Ahna:
Without you and without your love and support,
this project would not have seen the light of day.
Without your kindness, I would not
have the strength to be me.

A Simple Thank-you to:

Bev and Brock, "Stimpy", Laura, Sari, Trevor and Katharine, Bob, Geula, M, Glenda, T, Randi and Jordan, Skippy, Lady, Lee, Scott, Christa, Howard F., Cheryl, Arthur, Sharon, Bruce, Hennick, Mel and Chris, the spirit I knew as Sid Swerdlow, Mahmud, Marge, Steven, Debbie because she pushed me to do the readings, Joel, Howard, Rochelle, Mom and Dad, Jeffrey, Sammy, Sidney, Samantha, Taryn, Wyanne, Rob, Tracey, Jennifer, Gabi, Lee J., Don, BCSMSOSA, Dena, Patti, Tony J., Catherine, Lee Ann, Mahalia, The Spiritual Support Group, Wendy, Bill Courage, The Grateful Dead, Ami, Vincent, John, Paul, George and Ringo, Paul, Ace, Peter, Bruce, Eric, Eric, Tommy, Gene. A special thank-you to Mr. Paul Williams, whose poetry, music and blessings have moved me beyond measure.

Table of Contents

THE BIRTH

Dear Reader:

What you are about to read is on all counts an accurate description of what happened to me on three separate occasions in the early part of 1997, which directly preceded the birth of this book. You have no reason to believe me. The more you read this, the more far-fetched this may seem to you. I, on the other hand, have no reason to lie to you. I would not want to incur the Karma.

On the night of February 10th, 1997, I dreamt that I was in a large dark room that seemed to have neither beginning nor ending. All that was there was empty space, and yet I was not alone in it. With me was the strongest spiritual force that

I had ever encountered. I could feel Its presence. It felt like God. I looked down at my palms and discovered that they were bleeding. I looked up at God and asked, "How do I know that this is real?"

God replied, "Well, Joseph, you will never need a blood transfusion and your blood will always smell like roses."

I said, "Okay." Then I awoke.

The next day everything seemed okay. I didn't find any blood on my bed sheets, nor did I feel any different than I had the day before. In the afternoon, I took some time to sit quietly with my thoughts. Upon returning from my inner journey, I saw physically what some people would call a miracle. As I opened my eyes, I discovered I had a visitor. It wasn't just any ordinary being: it was the Blessed Virgin Mary.

To appreciate just how bizarre the dream and the vision were for me, you need to know that I am Jewish. I was born Jewish, raised Jewish and, in many respects, have remained connected to the religion throughout my adult life. I am also an intuitive and have witnessed some very unusual and spiritually fantastic things in my life and in my work, but seeing the energetic image of the Virgin Mary right in front of me was truly unreal. I could not believe my eyes. I rubbed them to see if she was real. She was.

She appeared to me as a completely transparent three-dimensional holographic image of a Saint. Being with her felt like being in the presence of purity, divinity and complete innocence simultaneously. I don't think I blinked for the whole time she was with me. All I could do was to stare at her. She, quite lovingly, stared back.

A few moments later she was gone. What amazed me was how non-sensational the experience seemed: no flash, no pomp and circumstance and no fear. All that remained after her departure was love.

Two months later, I had another profound vision. This one was again in my dream state. I dreamt that I was in an Orthodox Jewish synagogue wearing a tallis (a spiritual scarf). While I was praying in the sanctuary, a voice spoke to me that said, "Joseph, follow me." I left the sanctuary and followed the voice down a set of stairs that led me to the basement. When I got there, I found a long dark tunnel through which I was instructed to walk. On the other side of the tunnel was another staircase for me to climb up. When I reached the top, I found myself in a church sanctuary. Then I woke up.

These three experiences changed me internally in a very dramatic way. With my whole being, I understood that beneath all of our beliefs and practices, we are all inherently connected. Two to three days later, this book began its birthing process.

How this book wrote itself was incredible. Various expressions and sentences started to come to me at a rate that I could barely keep up with. I simply couldn't stop them. All of them seemed like one-line spiritual lessons complete on their own.

When these teachings would come in, I felt like I was getting smacked with a ball of energy that demanded I do something with them. Often these lessons would arrive at 2:00 in the morning, and when that happened, I would have to get out of bed, turn the lights on, go to the table, write down what was now inside of me, go back to bed only to get up and do it again moments later. This process continued for several months and resulted in the pages that follow.

The impact of witnessing myself go through this experience and absorbing what poured out of me was immeasurable. Just a few years before, I had been living a life that on the outside had everything. I worked in sales, following what I had been told to do in order to make a decent living. I was engaged to be married at the ripe age of 27, and I was an addict – addicted to escapism, food, cigarettes, sex and putting other people's needs too far ahead of my own. I had a personality that made it appear to others that everything was okay. Internally, however, I was in a constant state of misery and had a daily morning ritual of being in the shower and praying, "Why me, and when does my life get to begin?" What I didn't realize at the time was that living in this state was the result of an accumulation of years, since childhood, of being trained how NOT to listen to myself. I also didn't realize that this was an experience shared by many.

By the time this book arrived, I had already began my studies in mysticism and psychology and saw that different sects and philosophies all had different terms for what I was about to go through and in many respects had already begun. I had already left a life where I thought I knew love but was in fact empty. Now, I had to make the journey from illusion and suffering to a place of clarity and equanimity. This book and the ones that followed were the road maps I took to find myself.

I'm convinced the process of awakening is by far the most important and challenging process one can go through in life because it consists of the systematic breakdown of one's belief systems and forces a person to confront every nuance and discomfort he or she feels inside. As I myself continue to make my way through this process, this book still serves as my trusted companion offering me comfort, guidance and encouragement to keep moving forward.

Just as they did for me, I hope the words in this book will help you to work through the blocks that keep you from discovering your unique and perfect Self, one realization at a time, one insight at a time, at the pace you were simply meant to travel – your own.

Sincerely,

Joseph

ON
DREAMS

There is no graveyard for unrealized dreams.

The only thing that gets in the way of having your
innermost dreams manifested is you.

You, like every other individual, carry with you an important message needed by others. Expressing this message is critical for you to help others find their freedom. During this process, your own dreams, quite miraculously, become fulfilled.

Dreams, amongst other things, are conduits
to the Spirit world.

A life-long dream is Spirit's way of giving you direction. As you embark down that road, you become one with the Spirit of your dream. This very joining makes the dream manifest. It also teaches you about intimacy.

The realization of your dreams becomes
manifested primarily through patience,
endurance, compassion and dedication to serve
others via your vehicle of choice.

ON
FEAR & CONTROL

Behind every feeling of fear is a seed of love.

Each and every seed of love that is hidden in fear longs to reveal itself. Exposure of this seed is what allows it to blossom and thus become you.

Never stop the flow of creativity for the fear that reality will not accommodate it.

War and oppression
are faces of fear.

Violence is an expression of fear.

Life-defeating fear is a state we learn growing up.
We are not born with this conditioning.

Fear, when it is released, is replaced by love. The physical body needs love to return to its original state of balance so that healing can take place.

Often, the root of fear is an absence of knowledge, whether it is about yourself or the world.

Fear is an indication of the direction you are meant to walk so that you can find the light.

Integrity is the opposite of being a victim
to your fears.

The only method to release yourself from your
inner prison is to resolve your fears
of abandonment.

Denial is a mask worn by fear.

In order to befriend fear, you must consciously
feel it. Start with your most accessible.

Fears that are broken down and resolved lead to the resurrection of love, which becomes the rejuvenation of inner peace.

All control issues
are demonstrations of fear.

God will always have a resting place
for your control issues.

ON

MONEY & SUCCESS

Money does not lie awake at night
thinking about people!

All security that is purchased

is temporary.

A solid sense of Self cannot be bought.

The dollar bill has taken precedence over the bill
of human rights. It is for this reason that
two-income families have become the norm.

In order to understand the true value of a dollar,
you must be able to see beyond its physical value.

Success is an outgrowth of good communication
with yourself, others and that which inspires you.

Success is a natural state of being.

All brilliance requires love
and patience to blossom.

Without patience, there will be no success.

The art of being patient relies on wisdom
as its starting point.

The major ingredients needed in developing
patience are time, effort and,
most importantly, humility.

JOSEPH ELIEZER

Do what comes naturally to you. Ignore ideas that are not in harmony with your own unique vision.

A good business move is to prepare internally
for great business.

Success is the act of turning yesterday's
knowledge into wisdom that can be used
to better serve others today.

The leader must never become greater
than the vision.

You cannot ever fail. You can only give up trying, which results in a lack of manifesting.

Even the smallest vision takes consistent effort to take flight.

Staying connected to your kindness and
compassion is the best defence against misfortune.

The largest of doors opens when the past no
longer dominates your mind.

ON
LIFE

You only live once. At a time.

Growing is a reality of life. How you engage in it,
if at all, is a reflection of your integrity.

Life begins, and you become a product of your environment. Life evolves, and your environment becomes your product.

Very little has greater impact on your life than your own thoughts.

Life truly begins when you change your expectations from failure to success.

Love, water and intuition are the three major
ingredients with which all beings enter the world.

In every ONE lies a key to the Universe.

Collectively, we can unlock the whole.

The earth has consciousness. It thinks
in ways in which we have yet to evolve.

Karma is the spiritual term for
"what goes around, comes around,"
day after day, year after year, life after life.

If you wish to create better Karma for yourself,
all you need to do is examine
the intention behind each of your actions.

The key to developing self-respect
lies in embracing your heritage.

A family's lineage is invaluable. Without it,
one could not find the true source
of one's neurosis.

There is no life that has more blessings
than your own. If it feels like others' do,
you are not looking hard enough at yours.

ON
EATING DISORDERS
& BEAUTY

The roots of eating disorders
are planted in rage.

Eating disorders are non-verbal.

Comfort food is neither.

Recognizing beauty is an inside job.

54

There is no fragrance that is more potent or
intoxicating than your essence.

Beautiful is what the energy inside of you
looks like when manifested.

Feeling and expressing your uniqueness, your precious essence, allows others to see the Spirit in the flesh. It is this very expression that human beings see as being both beautiful and irresistible.

ON
RELATIONSHIPS
& SEXUALITY

Settling down with an unsuitable partner
will never result in the full unfolding
of potential for either party.

If your intuition tells you to leave a relationship
and you choose not to, you are prolonging your
destiny, which prevents better futures
for both you and your partner.

If you want to know a person's nature,

watch his or her behaviour

during an emotional crisis or conflict.

Staying in a loveless relationship
represents a fear of abandonment
shared by both parties.

Staying hooked on a past relationship
is symbolic of something within yourself
that needs attention.

When someone always needs to be right,

that person denies the wisdom in others.

This action creates a state of non-movement,

which leads to decay.

Healthy relationships require both parties to be healthy. You cannot have a healthy relationship with another person by yourself.

If you are in an abusive relationship and the person who is abusing you does not seek help, get help and get out!

To try to control your partner is to play God.

This particular play always ends in tragedy.

The family that plays together

is conscious.

In order to attract the best life partner,
you must first learn to honour yourself
fully, completely.

In order to develop trust in another, you must
first learn to trust yourself.

In order to love another, you must first learn self-love. Otherwise, what you perceive as love will turn out to be an unhealthy attachment.

Kindness is a gift you must consistently give to yourself in order to learn how to treat your partner appropriately.

Often, it is difficult to see why two people choose to be with each other when you look at them with your physical eyes only.

In order to see Spirit in all relationships, you must learn to see each and every being, including your enemy, with an open heart.

JOSEPH ELIEZER

Accepting Spirit into one's sex life supports
the BIG BANG theory of creation.

People who make love with others of the same
gender live with a special type of bravery. It is
quite possible that for this very reason
they bring up fear and anger in others.

If love and romance with people of the same sex
is a disease, then how fortunate are we to have
at least one major "ailment" that lists love for
another as its strongest symptom?

If we are all inherently connected,
then there is not one being who is not,
in some way, a soul mate.

A soul mate is a creation of the Divine
that is put on the planet to teach you.

JOSEPH ELIEZER

Soul mates come in all shapes, sizes,
cultures and ethnicity.

A soul mate does not have to be human.

Like with any intimate relationship, to maximize your relationship with your pet, you must be willing to share both your emotional and your physical space with it fully.

Your work life and your love life have much in common. In order to get the most from either, you must be willing to shed layers of pretence to get to your core values. This is the road that leads to the greatest rewards.

ON
LOVE & SELF-LOVE

Unexpected gifts are presents of love manifested.

Love uses perseverance as food.

JOSEPH ELIEZER

Love brings abundance of all kinds.

It knows no lack.

Love is treating yourself with kindness and
compassion when your mind is speaking
to you harshly.

Love has no private agenda and will
continuously present you with circumstances
that will challenge you.

Love never changes, only we do.

Love is the blueprint
on which all things are created.

The impact of true love blossoms over time.
It is a force that pulls and directs, revealing past
hurts that are brought to your attention so that
you can heal through them. Like with any good
recycling program, these wounds then become
converted into strengths, which help you
to realize love more deeply.

ON
EMOTIONAL HEALING

Sarcasm is hatred projected towards another.

Hatred towards another is a form of self-hatred.

Self-hatred is a manifestation of not being able to embrace your own uniqueness.

To speak negatively about someone or something
is an action that reveals your own hidden wounds.

A vice is a harmful tool used
to suppress your feelings.

Denial is a defensive state people use to protect
themselves from the impact of certain events.

The only zoo one ever needs to visit is one's mind.

When you remove an emotional blockage,
a flood of information arrives.

97

Self-reflection

gives birth to freedom.

Feeling and expressing your emotions

in a non-violent way is what carves the way

into and releases the Self.

Anger, when experienced consciously,
precipitates growth.

In order to attain greater inner stability,
you must first befriend instability.

Resolving emotional issues leads you to a place of
balance and integrity. This is the only place where
inner peace can be attained and maintained.

In order to become balanced, you must
be willing to relinquish all control
you perceive you have over others.

Taking yourself – your Self – into therapy is much like fixing a car. The process involves examining different aspects of the Self and then upgrading those parts as needed. If parts that need replacing are overlooked, your vehicle WILL smash into a wall.

The voices of anger and sabotage in your mind are strong, but they are not stronger than your connection to peace, which resurfaces as these voices are challenged and subsequently silenced.

The more you clear yourself emotionally,

the easier it is for you to live in

and cultivate harmony.

Your nature is shaped by an accumulation of lessons learned and the wisdom from those lessons internalized and actualized.

Underneath all of your wounds are seeds you are meant to plant and grow so that you may live in the garden of abundance. You are responsible for finding, planting and nourishing each seed.

Resolving your own personal conflicts is
the first step to ending global conflict.

All emotional healing journeys must include
a Spiritual component to be complete.

Emotions have no relationship to linear time.

Each and every new understanding you uncover
while you are searching for equanimity
is a cause for celebration.

ON

BEING IN THE WORLD

Be yourself. To not be you is to act according to someone else's idea of who you are and what you should be.

The only control you have in life lies in the process with which you make your own decisions.

The truth is never far:
It is always inside of you.

You will never lose sight
of what is most important when you are coming
from a place of honesty.

Once you have resolved much of your past and
have cultivated the strength and self-esteem
to face your future, the true gift of being in the
present unfolds. And that is the realization of
knowing NOW is all there is.

The key to opening yourself lies in your
willingness to do so.

The key to remaining positive
is to stay true and act according to
what you feel inside.

Optimism,
no matter how dark the moment,
is a choice.

The kindest gifts you can give to another are forgiveness and understanding.

If there is no choice but to be violent,
think again.

The best response to an insult is love.

The mother of all cures is forgiveness.

ON
INTUITION

Intuition is the best and most accurate tool
you have to identify the presence of Spirit
in your life.

To not follow your intuition is to decline an invitation sent by Spirit for greater intimacy between yourself and the Universe.

To follow your intuition always, regardless of
what life looks like to you at the moment,
is a sign of Self-mastery.

To work with intuition fully, you must develop
the clarity to listen and the courage to act.

In order to intuit life fully,
you must first get INTO it.

Intuition works best, initially, when presented with yes or no questions.

Intuition fills you with light when all is a go.
Don't second-guess it.

Intuition fills you with a feeling of heaviness
when it is trying to tell you not to proceed.

If after taking a risk, you receive a rush
of new realizations, it is your confirmation
you have made the best decision.

Intuition does not lie.

To not follow your intuition
is to refuse help from Spirit.

Not trusting your intuition
is your way of telling Spirit
that you are more insightful than It is.

JOSEPH ELIEZER

To not follow your intuition is manipulation of
your destiny. This self-betrayal never
brings positive results.

People often fail to heed their intuition out of fear of what life might look like if they do. Acting on intuition in the face of fear brings the most unexpected rewards.

In order to see Spirit in every one and every thing,
it is important to dedicate your life
to being lived intuitively.

The secret to living the life you have always
dreamed of lies in trusting your intuition
consistently to get you there.

One of the earliest intuitive feelings you will receive is that you have had a past life.

Intuition tells you immediately when you are
experiencing a moment filled with destiny.

Destiny confirms itself
as an inner sense of knowing.

Intuition is the seed
from which all talent is born.

ON
FAITH, RELIGION
& SPIRITUALITY

There is no Viagra or Cialis for faith.

Faith is a term used for people who make the leap
into a new reality and trust that Spirit
will catch them.

Spirituality needs to replace religion. As this is accomplished, the reality All is One will be the basis on which all society will rebuild itself.

Religious holidays must first be internalized for them to be understood as Spiritual holidays.

As society transforms, the names of the holy virtues will be transformed from Faith, Hope and Charity to Faith, Hope and Clarity.

One of the key elements in the development of faith comes by dealing with, and subsequently giving up, your control issues.

The essence of spirituality is the elimination of hierarchy so that we are able to see the sameness in all beings and Spirit in all things.

There is no hierarchy on the way to heaven.

If there were, we would not be able

to embrace the teaching All is One.

Living by way of Spiritual guidance
may not give you worldly security,
but it will release you of INsecurity.

It is necessary to develop
your sense of integrity to realize divinity.

JOSEPH ELIEZER

There is no evil.

There is only confused good.

ON
ELEMENTS OF THE
SPIRITUAL JOURNEY

Most Spiritual and healing journeys
begin as crises.

The greater your commitment to the process
of developing your Spiritual Self,
the more fulfilling your journey will be.

Any discomfort you feel in your physical life (for example, not happy with money, relationships or status) is a reflection of an area within yourself where your relationship with Self, and ultimately with Spirit, needs attention.

All you are is what gets discovered
through the Spiritual healing journey.

Growing into yourself often requires
you to become estranged,
even if just temporarily, from society.

Thoughts of suicide on the Spiritual healing journey are NORMAL. Just do not act on them.

Starting off on your Spiritual journey often requires you to leave the familiar behind. You will probably feel either forced or compelled to do this. This departure is usually the first step on the pathway of coming home.

You know that you hit a benchmark on your Spiritual journey when your concern over your Karmic debt outweighs the concern over your credit card debt.

Releasing emotional blocks, the cornerstone of the Spiritual journey, often drains the Self of physical energy... which is later restored.

Living a Spiritual life very often requires you to leave your past behind in order to obtain your future in the present. This journey must be taken one step at a time and, in order to be precise, must be done intuitively.

Your Spiritual journey is mirrored in your garden,
representing the eternal Spiritual truths
of birth and re-birth.

Your moods, while you travel along the path of
Spiritual growth and enlightenment, can swing
like pendulums. You need to develop an extreme
amount of awareness and patience in order to not
act them out. As you cultivate these strengths,
you discover what it is to be centred.

ON
ILLUSION & CLARITY

Illusion is what prevents you from knowing and
experiencing Spirit and Self.

The perception that Spirit is not with you 24
hours a day is an illusion. Don't buy into it.

Power is one of life's biggest illusions.

Sincerity brings clarity.

Without clarity, there cannot be fulfillment.

The clearer you become, the easier it is
to obtain even greater clarity.

The more clarity you attain within yourself,
the greater the contribution to society
you can make.

A mistake is what happens
when one perceives and acts without clarity.
That is why it is called a mis-take.

The only time you feel blocked from receiving

messages, signs or Spiritual guidance is when you

are insistent on having your own way.

Letting go of that kind of mentality

is what brings you clarity.

Spiritual knowledge becomes wisdom
through spurts of insightful clarity.

The desire to get closer to Spirit
forces you to find clarity.

The seeds of enlightenment are buried
under your negative thoughts and habits.

Enlightenment reveals itself
as you cleanse yourself of emotional
and mental debris.

A simple formula for enlightenment is:

you as you already are

– (minus) your illusions

= (equals) enlightenment.

JOSEPH ELIEZER

Enlightenment is not a destination.
It is an ongoing process
of Self-examination leading
to greater Self-understanding.

Enlightenment is not a race to the top, but an
experience that happens at your own speed.

Consider the tool often recommended by therapists. Whenever you enter an argument with someone, change the words "I blame you/You are...." to "When you do _____, I feel _____, and it makes me want to _____." Then wait for a reply. The results of this action alone will bring enlightenment to both parties.

JOSEPH ELIEZER

Enlightenment is a natural human experience.
It's okay to indulge.

When you act without integrity, you will feel a
loss of energy through your stomach. Reversing
your action(s) is what restores your energy and
gives birth to enlightenment.

Awareness brings enlightenment

brings awareness....

Enlightenment is not a prerequisite to having Spiritual gifts. It is a journey that must be taken by you who already has them.

In order to reach a place of harmony within the Self and the Universe, your dream, waking and intuitive states must all work in unison.

Experiencing divinity requires emotional availability and flexibility.

Emotional pain experienced during the process of becoming enlightened is often the result of new knowledge being born into consciousness, which is more appropriate than that which was previously seen as real.

ON
BEING TESTED BY SPIRIT
& JUDGEMENT DAY

Spirit does not test us.

Being tested by Spirit is an illusion,
plain and simple.

The only time you feel like Spirit is testing you
is when you are being asked to give up
some form of control.

Spirit does not punish.

JOSEPH ELIEZER

Judgment Day is the day
you become morally responsible.

Judgment Day is the day
you decide to confront your addictions.

Judgment Day is the day
you decide to stop acting out violently
in thought, word or deed.

To live with the notion Judgment Day is coming
is an action that keeps us living in fear.
We are not meant to live this way!

How can Judgment Day be a valid concept if we are all one? Wouldn't that one judgment from the Divine then speak for us all?

QUESTIONS
& PONDERINGS

How can the Spiritual world become integrated
into your physical life if you have not learned
to acknowledge and obey your intuition?

How omnipresent can Spirit be in your life if you
have not developed the wisdom
or cultivated the grace to accept it?

Why do so many people
go to Spiritual institutions only to be told
that the answers lie within?

What good is listening to and praying for
guidance if you lack the courage to act on it?

What good is a gift from Spirit if you do not learn
or have the patience to develop it so that you can
share it with others?

What good is searching for signs from Spirit if
you are not engaged in cultivating stillness
and openness to receive them?

Who and what thoughts hinder you from
allowing your vision to manifest?

If it is true that we all have abandonment issues,

then none of us is truly alone.

If Spirit is in every living thing, then it is
impossible to be alive without it.

If the devil is in the details,

where is the Divine?

It has been said that religion is the true source of all addiction. If this is true, then is it because it is lacking in Spirit?

JOSEPH ELIEZER

If repetition is the mother of skill, then
persistence must be its father!

If the human body is the temple of the living God,
then the local fitness centre and the grocery store
should be considered as places of worship.

PREDICTIONS

As society becomes more enlightened,

the concept of an eye for an eye

will be viewed as unacceptable by all.

As humankind evolves, clear or confused will replace the concept of right or wrong just as life-affirming or self-deprecating will take the place of the notions of good and bad.

The next step in the evolutionary process of humanity will be marked by emotional upheaval. This next step has already begun.

There will come a time, perhaps as you read this, when becoming a shepherd will again become a prosperous business.

The fear of an anti-Christ will cease as
humankind discovers and actualizes the
perception that God is within.

The need for politicians will end only when
all humankind can honour freedom
and compassion above all.

The next step up on the evolutionary ladder of pet medicine will be found through chiropractic care and acupuncture. It has already begun!

When humankind develops the sensitivity to and learns how to interrupt self-defeating or negative thought, all self-inflicted suffering will perish.

JOSEPH ELIEZER

ON
SPIRIT

Spirit communicates with every ONE.

Recognizing signs from Spirit is a very deep and personal experience. Spirit communicates in a language that only you can identify through an inner sense of knowing.

Deciphering messages from Spirit is a full-time job. The more experience you have with it, the more skilful you become.

One of the first ways people key into communication from Spirit is through a digital clock: 1:11, 2:22, 4:44, 11:11, etc. Spirit will have you look at the clock at these times, in various ways, as a way of acclimatizing you to its presence.

A coincidence is Spirit's way of giving you direct confirmation that you are on track in your life. Never discount it.

A bad vibe is a sign from Spirit telling you to change your direction or approach.

Not following signs from Spirit, or dismissing them as chance, prolongs the process of reaching fulfillment.

Animals are like Spirit in the way they communicate. Both send clear and distinct messages that can only be obscured or distorted through the recipient's self-doubt.

To be able to grasp some of the infinite number of ways in which Spirit communicates, you must be willing to face and dismantle your trust issues. Lack of trust distorts your connection.

The authentication of your own connection to Spirit cannot be fully realized until you start to trust and believe in your own insights.

To rely on Spirit as your teacher, you must learn to be grounded and develop the ability to live according to your own perception of truth.

The way of Spirit is to bring light into darkness:
finding wisdom in places within you, where
currently there is confusion, doubt or suffering.

Ask for one-on-one dialogue with the Divine and
ye shall receive. Just ask.

JOSEPH ELIEZER

To discover Spirit in all its splendour requires you
to resolve your fears and misconceptions.

Spirit teaches us how to be human.

Your deepest and truest expressions of Self and
the nature of Spirit are one and the same.

Spirit does not know, nor does it understand, the concept of abandonment.

Spirit does not end. And neither do you.

Two main reasons one turns to Spirit are
inspiration and desperation.

There is no such thing as
unnecessary Spiritual guidance.

Spirit is the lifeblood of uniqueness.

Your true relationship to Spirit can only be
revealed through time.

With Spirit as your master, you receive and give
all of who you are, one piece at a time.

All Spiritual truths incorporated into the Self
alter and deepen your connection to the Divine
and all its creation and to your awareness that
you are not separate from any one thing.

The perceived distance between yourself and Spirit consists of emotional and intellectual blockages that are necessary for your stability. Without them, you would go mad. Yet, you must dismantle them to bring your Self closer to Spirit. The only way this can be accomplished is one perception at a time.

You are, just as you are, truly beautiful.

About the Author

Joseph Eliezer is an intuitive, psychotherapist and author. He practises a unique form of therapy, called Intuition-Enhanced Psychotherapy, which combines Joseph's highly developed innate intuitive abilities with his counselling and psychotherapy training. As an intuitive psychotherapist, Joseph helps his clients bring clarity and understanding to their unique circumstances, gain insight into troubling situations and find solutions to many of life's puzzles.

From 1994 through 2004, Joseph (using the stage name of Lorne T Psychic) had regular segments on top-ranked radio and TV shows in the Vancouver, BC, area – CFOX 99.3 FM, *Day Time* on Shaw Cable and MOJO 730 AM *Talk Radio for Guys*. He has also made guest appearances on other stations and been interviewed for numerous print and on-line publications. Joseph's articles have been widely published, and he was a columnist for *Real West Magazine* for two years. His popular website is www.1111spiritroad.com.

Joseph lives in Vancouver, BC, with his partner Ahna.

9 781897 435427